Order this book online at www.trafford.com
or email orders@trafford.com

Most Trafford titles are also available at major online book retailers.

Printed in the United States of America.

ISBN: 978-1-4907-1629-9 (sc)
ISBN: 978-1-4907-1628-2 (e)

Library of Congress Control Number: 2013918274

Trafford rev. 10/01/2013

 www.trafford.com
North America & international
toll-free: 1 888 232 4444 (USA & Canada)
fax: 812 355 4082

THE ASPIRING ARCHITECT

AN ACTIVITY BOOK FOR KIDS

TRAVIS KELLY WILSON

Credits

Cover Design By Travis Wilson
Cover Illustration By Miacharro | Dreamstime.com

Key: T = Top, M = Middle, B = Bottom

CITY IDENTIFICATION ON EACH PAGE

Page - City, State and or Country
3. Chicago, Illinois, USA
4. Athens, Greece
5. Moscow, Russia
6. Rome, Italy
7. Warsaw, Poland
8. Istanbul, Turkey
9. Seattle, Washington, USA
10. London, England
11. Athens, Greece
12. Rome, Italy
13. Stockholm, Sweden
14. Barcelona, Spain
15. Budapest, Hungary
16. Vienna, Austria
17. Sydney, New South Wales, Australia
18. Rotterdam, Netherlands
19. Copenhagen, Denmark
21. Venice, Italy
22. New York City, New York, USA
23. Venice, Italy
24. Paris, France
25. Saint Louis, Missouri, USA
26. Copenhagen, Denmark
27. Kuala Lumpur, Malaysia
28. Beijing, China
31. Vienna, Austria
32. London, England,
33. Prague, Czech Republic
34. Florence, Italy
36. Sydney, New South Wales, Australia
37. London, England
38. Atlanta, Georgia, USA
42. Colonge, Germany
43. Venice, Italy
44. Munich, Germany
45. Tokyo, Japan
46. Houston, Texas, USA
47. Singapore, Republic of Singapore, City State
48. Barcelona, Spain

Recognizing Architecture

Architecture is one of the greatest arts. Each structure is a monument that identifies civilizations of the past and present. The understanding of past forms helps us understand how people have progressed over thousands of years. These forms are expressed in monuments, paintings, sculptures, and buildings. After viewing all these pieces of history, art, and science we can identify each culture through their buildings. People see the Parthenon as a symbol of ancient Greece. Everyone recognizes the Colloseum in Rome as the main sport facility of the Roman Empire. Recognizing the basic forms will help in understanding more about our architectural history and where we might be going in the future.

Enjoy all architecture; Past, Present, and Future,

TRAVIS KELLY WILSON

ARCHITECTURE

MEANS

THE PROFESSION OF DESIGNING AND

CONSTRUCTING A BUILDING

THE WORD ARCHITECTURE COMES FROM THE
LATIN WORD

ARCHITECTURA AND THE GREEK WORD

ARKHITEKTON

You pick the colors

Saint Basil's Cathedral, Moscow, Russia. This cathedral was built by Ivan the Terrible. It was built in six years from 1556 to 1561 to commerate the capture of Kazan and Asktrakhan.

FACTS OF THE FIRST BUILDINGS

Draw a line from each fact to the correct building.

Gladiators battled here for over 400 years.

Built with 2.5 million blocks weighing 2 1/2 tons.

It was designed to hold 50,000 people.

Has a hole in the roof called an oculus.

Contains three orders of columns: Doric, Ionic, and Corinthian

Had the largest concrete dome for almost 1400 years.

DO I USE ALL OF THESE BUILDINGS?

Architects throughout time have designed buildings for a specific purpose. Many buildings were for the Gods of Greece. Several were built for Kings and Queens. Today building are built for everyone to use. Do you ever use these buildings? Find and circle the building type in the word search.

```
C H L H K K S M V O
A O A O T X K U D N
S U R S N W Y E L N
T S D P T L S S O R
L E E I Q C C U O A
E M H T A U R M H B
D G T A O Z A K C U
X I A L I M P Z S A
W F C N Z I E J H A
E L P M E T R F T J
```

WORD BANK

Barn	Hospital	School
Castle	House	Skyscraper
Cathedral	Museum	Temple

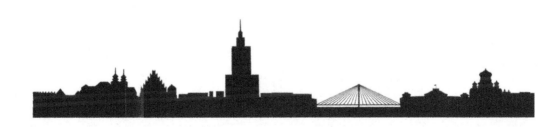

5

STYLE OF STRUCTURES

An architectural style is listed. Your challenge is to match with the appropriate building with the correct architectural style.

A. Gothic

B. Byzantine

C. Greek

D. Roman

TOOLS OF THE TRADE

If you were going to build a house what construction materials would you use. Circle the parts that were needed in building your house.

Computers
Papers
Copiers
Bricks
Steel
Lumber
Concrete
Stone
Wire
Pipes
Glass
Nails
Screws
Glue
Flooring

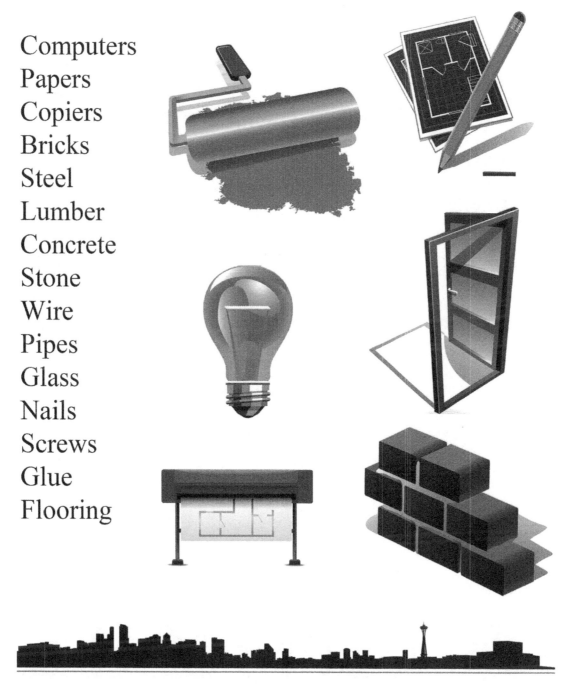

NAME THAT
EUROPEAN STRUCTURE

Structures are built in all different shapes and sizes. Draw a line to the correct picture.

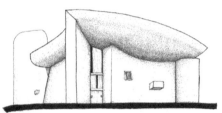

Eiffel Tower

Notre Dame du Haut

Týn Church

Tower of London

Leaning Tower of Pisa

TIMELINE
FIRST ARCHITECTS
MATCH THE ARCHITECT TO THEIR BUILDING
IMHOTEP, ICTINUS AND CALLICRATES, EMPEROR HADRIAN

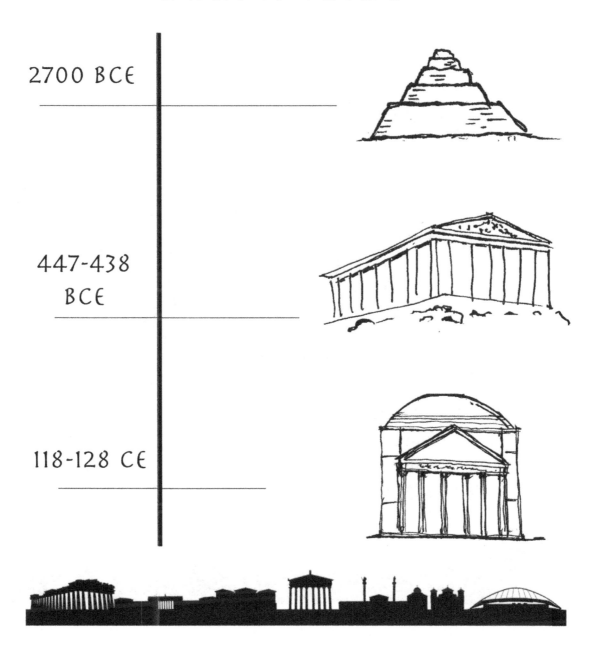

2700 BCE

447-438 BCE

118-128 CE

THERE'S A HOLE IN THE ROOF!

PANTHEON
Rome, Italy

Built: 118-127 CE

Facts: 1. The oldest completely intact building in the world.
2. Commissioned and partly designed by Emperor Hadrian.
3. Lets light in through a hole in the roof called an oculus.
4. Largest dome on the planet for almost 1400 years.

Are We Changing Styles Again?

Throughout the history of architecture new styles emerge. People are always looking for the newest and coolest style of the time. However, in the past, the styles did not change as fast as they do today. The Gothic style was used for most Catholic Cathedrals for 800 years. We are still designing building in the Greek styles and that was 2500 years ago.

```
E E B A Z C Q P M G E G
M C O A N R A V F O U N
Z L N B R V W W W T Q U
C Y O A D O R Z M H S V
P B D Q S O Q U L I E V
F P H J C S I U R C N H
D G A O J T I Z E A A D
D K C K N Y Z A K H M H
K O D A K B R M N U O R
V M Z B P K Y K E E R G
C Y H E R F H J Q C R T
B P A L L A D I A N S K
```

Baroque	Gothic	Palladian	Rococo
Byzantium	Greek	Renaissance	Romanesque

NAME THE PARTS OF THE CATHEDRAL

The Christian cathedral is originally based on the Roman basilicas form. The Roman Basilica was used as a public building normally within the Forum. The Forum was the main section of the city that contained the commercial, government, and religious structures. The cathedral evolved over the centuries, but retained the Roman forms of the nave, aisle, and apse

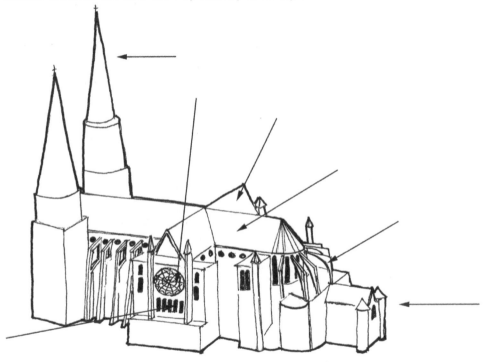

WORD BANK: Spire, Nave, Rose Window, Apse, Transept, Buttress, Triforium

WHERE DOES EVERYONE WORSHIP?

Everyone that practices a religion has a central gathering place. Architecture has been important to the idenities of religions. Each religion has a distinct style that is shown in their buildings.

Match the building with the identifying religion

Christianity, Islam, Buddhism, Hinduism, Judism

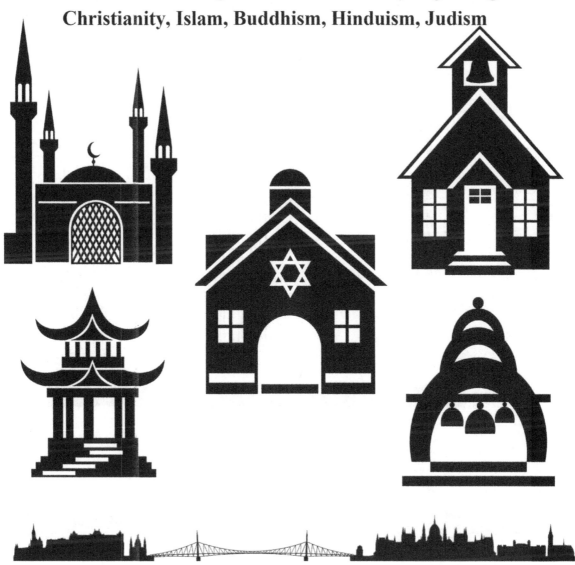

NAME THAT COLUMN

WORD BANK
Ionic, Corinthan, Doric

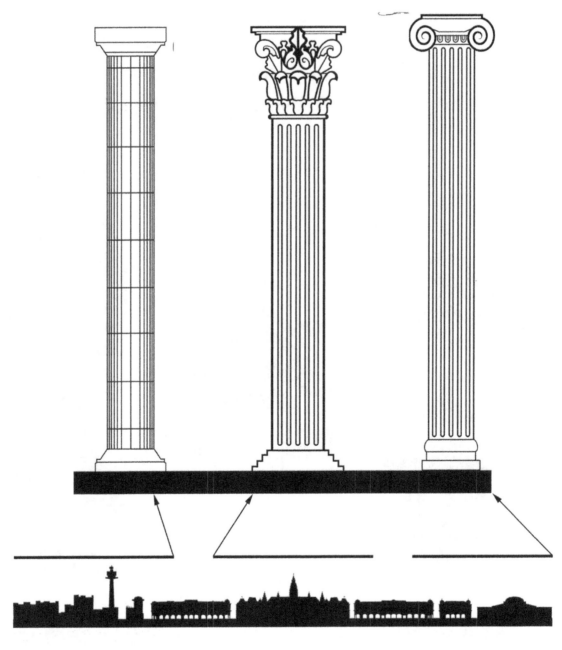

NAME THAT ARCHITECT

Architects are the primary designers of buildings today. Most architects design using certain building styles that clients recognize and select based on personal preference.

Research an architect and provide a short biography.

Select An Architect

Architect _____

Frank Lloyd Wright
Mies van der Rohe
Le Corbusier
Eero Saarinen
Louis Kahn
I. M. Pei
Michael Graves
Richard Mieier
Richard Rogers
Norman Foster
Renzo Piano

Paste a picture of the architects work.

Biography of the architect

_____
_____
_____
_____

List interesting facts about the architect and their famous buildings.

_____
_____
_____

WHERE ARE WE AT?

Find the country where each structure is located

A. Stonehenge   B. Great Wall   C. Hagia Sofia
D. Castillo   E. Louvre   F. Golden Gate

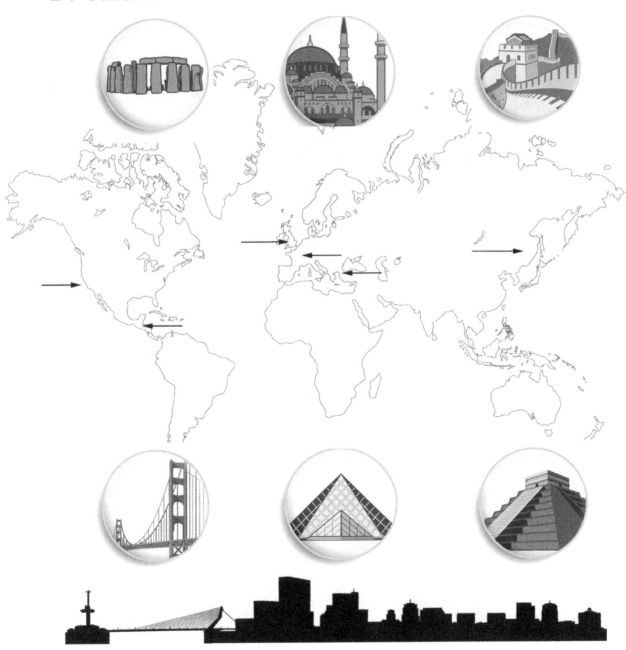

MODERN PILGRIMAGE CHAPEL
NOTRE-DAME DU HAUT
LOCATED IN RONCHAMP, FRANCE

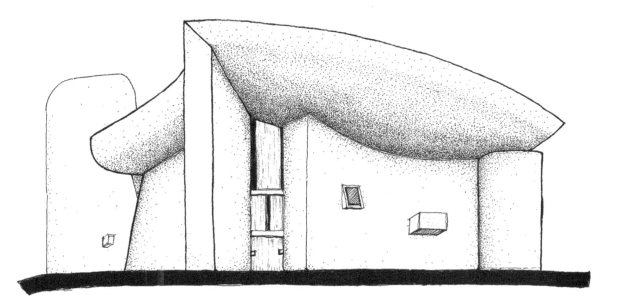

Architect: Le Corbusier
Date Completed: 1955

The chapel is the third on the site. The first was built in the 4th century and the second was destroyed during WWII.

The chapel's interior is flooded with light from stained glass windows in walls up to ten feet thick.

The roof resembles a nuns habit. The concrete roof stands on small steel rods. This allows light to flow under the roof and above the wall. On bright days, the roof appears to be floating.

During rainstorms, water flows off the roof and creates water fountains.

If I become a building professional what would I be?

Architect   Contractor   Engineer
Interior Designer Carpenter   Mason
Electrician   Plumber   Decorator

Pick three career paths and describe their jobs.

1. _____

_____

2. _____

_____

3. _____

_____

I LOVE SYMMETRY

Symmetry means equally divided or balanced.

Villa Capra or La Rotonda
Architect: Andrea Palladio

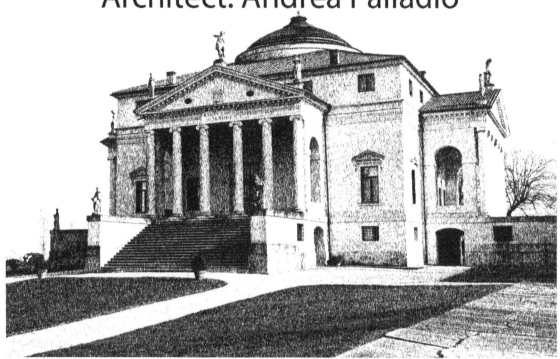

This building has four identical sides. It has a center dome which was the first for a house. The interior rooms were designed with one room proportion to the next. Each larger room is connected to one that is half its size. Proportion is the proper balance of objects .

Built: 1567-1593
Location: Vicenza, Italy

What kind of building am I?

A	B	C	D	E	F	G	H	I	J	K	L	M	N	O
1	2	3	4	5	6	7	8	9	10	11	12	13	14	15

P	Q	R	S	T	U	V	W	X	Y	Z
16	17	18	19	20	21	22	23	24	25	26

1. I can be all different sizes and my choir raises the roof.

___ ___ ___ ___ ___ ___ ___ ___ ___
3 1 20 8 5 4 18 1 12

2. When the wind blows I get the SHAKES!

___ ___ ___ ___ ___ ___ ___ ___ ___ ___
19 11 25 19 3 18 1 16 5 18

3. Children are always reading, writing, and running in me.

___ ___ ___ ___ ___ ___
19 3 8 15 15 12

4. I wish those senators would stop leaving messes at my desks.

___ ___ ___ ___ ___ ___ ___
3 1 16 9 20 1 12

Would everyone stop copying me?

Andrea Palladio (1508-1580)

Palladio was an Italian Renassiance architect that designed using the building styles of ancient Greece and ancient Rome. He started as a bricklayer, then became a humanist scholar, then finally an architect. A humanist scholar is a person that studies human nature and their values. As an architect Palladio revived the classical style. His designs led to most public, government, and financial building becoming classical in style for over 400 years. It is now called Palladian. Every time you see a government building or a bank with columns and a half round window you can thank Palladio.

Just call me T.J.

Thomas Jefferson (1743-1826) had many interests. He was a farmer, inventor, philosopher, ambassador to France, architect, and third President of the United States. Jefferson believed his designs reflected that of the Roman Republic and would give stability to the new American Republic. Many of his buildings reflected the works of Palladio. Monticello, his home, is a symmetrical building with a central dome resembling the buildings of Palladio. He brought neoclassical design to the United States.

Places To Go and People To See

If you were living during the time periods you might have made these statements.

Word Bank

Chicago   St. Mark's   Eiffel

Nîmes   Pisa   Moscow

Great Wall   Egypt   Ethiopia

Rome

1. You could see the tallest building in the United States from my _____ bedroom.

2. When visiting the great pyramids you need to travel to Giza, _____.

3. I visited _____ square and got to play with pigeons.

4. Once I rode an elevator in the _____ Tower and could see all of Paris.

5. I walked thousands of miles on the _____ of China.

6. I once fought to the death at the Colosseum in _____.

7. Once Ivan the Terrible told me he would poke out my eyes if I built any thing as beautiful as St. Basils in _____.

8. I forgot to dig the foundation deep enough and that bell tower is leaning pretty badly in _____, Italy.

9. We were digging and digging and all of a sudden we had built the Rock Church of Saint George in Lalibela, _____.

10. I once rode my swimming float 25 miles on the Pont du Gard going to _____, France.

Crossing the World

MONTICELLO

Pantheon

BAUHAUS

Versailles

PARTHENON

PETRA

Across

3) Home of the Treasury
5) German School of International Design
6) Thomas Jefferson spent 40 years building

Down

1) Greek standard of design
2) Home of King Louis XIV
4) Hole in the roof

NAME THAT ASIAN STRUCTURE

Asia is a large expanse of land with a wide variety of cultures. The structures of Asia are built with various purposes and many different materials. Draw a line connecting the structure to their intended purpose.

The Great Wall of China

HOUSING, SCHOOL, RELIGIOUS CENTER

Taj Mahal

DEFENSE

TEMPLE / TOMB

Lingaraja Temple

The Treasury

MEMORIAL / TOMB

ARCHITECTURAL CAPITALS

```
A W K C Q Y Q L N O D M G R
R M T B A D N O X I T M E K
W A S H I N G T O N L U I X
O T N N Z U B U Y I G R E S
C B M U Z S I E Y A R W E W
S N O D N O L O R B M O G B
O Y N C C T B P T R A T M L
M V K U A E E H U A A G W E
H U T I I J O P R S A P V Y
K B R J Y E A N B I W M H D
K B I N Z L C C M L L Z D K
S N E S R L T S N I O P B H
G A H C B I V F P A R I S U
J G P S I N S V Y V H T F Z
```

Beijing	Brasilia	London	Paris	Rome
Berlin	Canberra	Moscow	Prague	Washington

26

GRAND BUILDINGS

Words in each line are merged together. Find the orginal words.

MaThaajl
India
☐☐☐ ☐☐☐☐☐

HSagophiiaa
Turkey
☐☐☐☐☐ ☐☐☐☐☐☐

SaPetienrts
Rome
☐☐☐☐☐ ☐☐☐☐☐

EmSptiartee
New York
☐☐☐☐☐☐ ☐☐☐☐

CHhoiussweick
England
☐☐☐☐☐☐☐ ☐☐☐☐☐

BHioltumorsee
North Carolina
☐☐☐☐☐☐☐ ☐☐☐☐☐

DID YOU KNOW SKYSCRAPERS MOVE IN THE WIND?

Skyscrapers can move a couple of feet depending on their height and construction materials. Over the last 100 years engineers have developed many construction methods and equipment to stabilize the building. The first skyscrapers were welded extremely tight to reduce the sway. The next group worked around a strong central steel core that connected into the frame. Today, many buildings are built with a super strong reinforced concrete core in the center. Some skyscrapers use a tuned mass damper which has a huge weight that shifts back and forth high in the building. As the wind pushes one direction the weight shifts to stabilize the building.

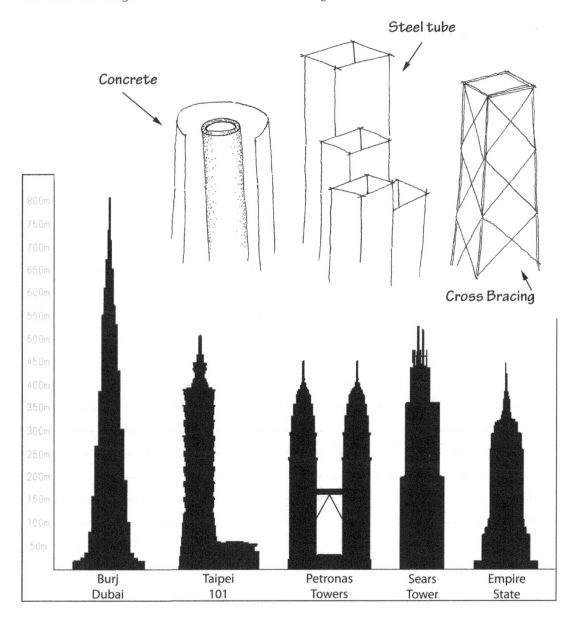

Concrete

Steel tube

Cross Bracing

Let's Play Follow The Leader

Chartres Cathedral in France has a Labyrinth inlaid in the floor.
A labyrinth is like a maze but has only one path from entry to
exit. A maze is a game that makes you search for the correct
path. Chartres labyrinths has been used as paths for prayer on
one's knees.

I'm trapped and I can't get OUT!

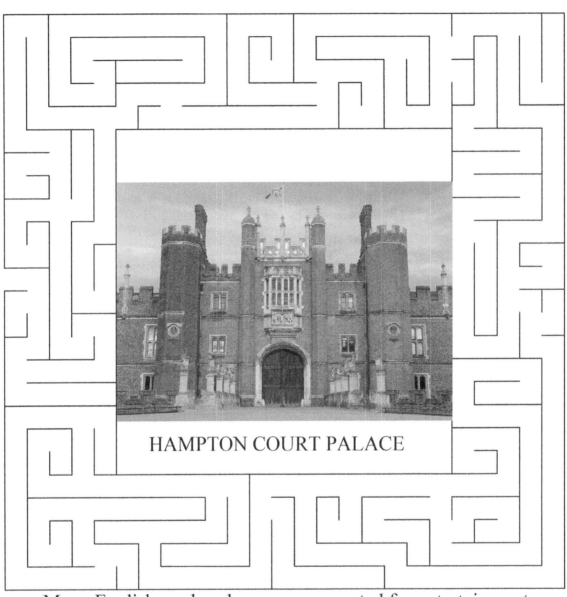

HAMPTON COURT PALACE

Many English gardens have mazes created for entertainment.
The oldest surviving hedge maze is at Hampton Court Palace.
It was created for King William III in the 17th century.

I'm a SPY. I only write secret CRYPTOGRAMS.

Decode the message by finding each substitute letter or symbol.

A	B	C	D	E	F	G	H	I	J	K	L	M	N	O	P	Q	R	S	T	U	V	W	X	Y	Z
2	12	26	3	25	11	7	10	14	6	4	17	1	5	16	18	9	23	13	8	24	19	15	21	22	20

__ __ __ __   __ __   __ __ __ __
17 25 13 13   14 13   1 16 23 25

A	B	C	D	E	F	G	H	I	J	K	L	M	N	O	P	Q	R	S	T	U	V	W	X	Y	Z
13	17	16	23	10	9	1	25	24	21	22	3	12	4	7	20	2	5	26	6	15	8	19	14	18	11

__ __ __   __ __   __ __   __ __ __   __ __ __ __ __ __ __ .
1 7 23   24 26   24 4   6 25 10   23 10 6 13 24 3 26

Mies van der Rohe was a early designer of the modern glass skyscraper. He immigrated to the United States after the Nazi's closed the Bauhaus school of design. He then lead the Armour Institute which became the Illinois Institute of Technology (IIT).

WHAT ARE THE PARTS OF A COLUMN

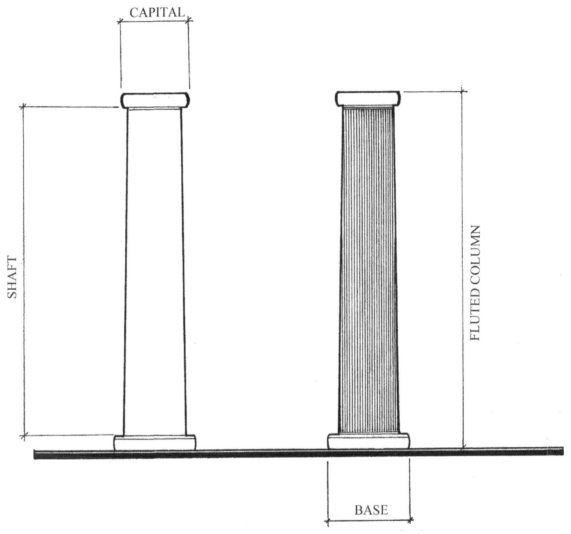

Columns have three parts: base, shaft, and capital. Columns were originally made of wood. The Greeks and Romans produced them in stone. Now, we produce columns out of steel, aluminum, fiberglass, and even plastic. Most columns are tapered, which means they are smaller at the top than the bottom. However, many ancient temples actually made them larger at the top and smaller at the bottom. This gave the optical illusion that the columns were the same size when standing and looking up at the temple.

I COMMAND YOU TO COLOR THE ANCIENT PYRAMIDS OF EGYPT!

FACTS:
The Great Pyramid of Egypt is located in the town of El Giza.
It was the burial tomb for the Sun God Khufu.
It is the oldest existing Seven Wonders of the Ancient World.
It took 20 years to build and completed 2560 BC.

I Like to Sing and Dance
Sydney Opera House

Sydney, New South Wales, Australia

ARCHITECT: JORN UTZON

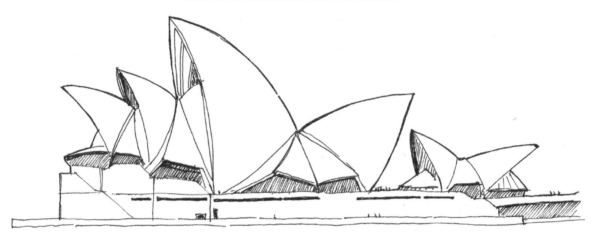

Many people think it resembles ship sails while others mention sea shells. The roof shells were created from cutting a sphere into pieces. It was the most controversial building in Australia. The architect and government battled over the design until he quit. He never saw the building after leaving in 1966. However, in 1999, Jorn Utzon was rehired to develop the design principles for the future of the opera house, but still never returned to Australia.

Facts: The roof is covered with over 1,000,000 ceramic tiles.
The grand organ contains over 10,500 pipes.
Designed -1957, Opened - 1973, Start of remodel - 2001

Do I become a scientist or an architect?
Sir Christopher Wren
1632-1723

Sir Christopher Wren had many interests in his life. Early in his life, he was an astronomy professor. He was one of the founding members of the Royal Society. The Royal Society was one of the earliest organizations dedicated to all things science and mathematics. Other members of the Royal Society were physicist Sir Isaac Newton, the philosopher Robert Hooke, and inventor Robert Boyle.

After The Great Fire of 1666, Wren focused on the rebuilding of London. He completed hospitals, the Royal Observatory, Kensington Palace, additions to Hampton Court, and designed over 50 churches.

FLOORPLANS

Architects design buildings for clients. Clients are people that hire architects to design a building to their needs and preferences. An architect meets with their new client to develop a program. The program is all the information needed to design the building exactly like the client wants and meets all the building health and safety codes.

Your challenge is to make a short program for a house and draw a basic floor plan based on your requirements. Make a list of all the rooms you would need in your house.

ROOMS

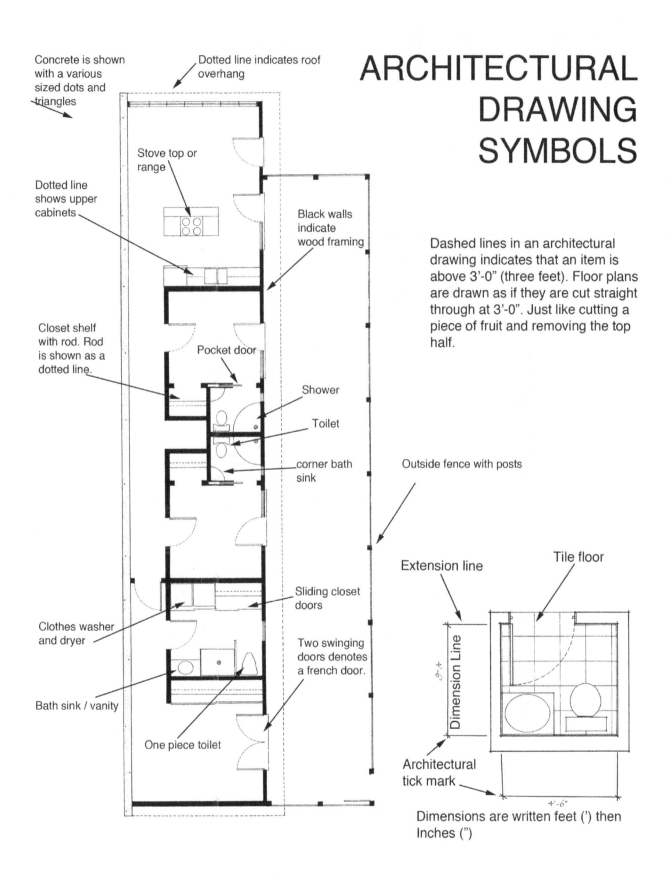

ARCHITECTURAL DRAWING SYMBOLS

Concrete is shown with a various sized dots and triangles

Dotted line indicates roof overhang

Stove top or range

Dotted line shows upper cabinets

Black walls indicate wood framing

Dashed lines in an architectural drawing indicates that an item is above 3'-0" (three feet). Floor plans are drawn as if they are cut straight through at 3'-0". Just like cutting a piece of fruit and removing the top half.

Closet shelf with rod. Rod is shown as a dotted line.

Pocket door

Shower

Toilet

corner bath sink

Outside fence with posts

Extension line

Tile floor

Dimension Line

4'-0"

Sliding closet doors

Clothes washer and dryer

Two swinging doors denotes a french door.

Bath sink / vanity

Architectural tick mark

4'-6"

One piece toilet

Dimensions are written feet (') then Inches (")

SAMPLE FLOOR PLAN

Below is a sample apartment floorplan. It has been sketched to show locations of the main living spaces. Notice the bathroom and kitchen symbols. The symbols show the location of the sinks, stove, refrigerator, bathtub, and toilet. The last few symbols are the doors and windows.

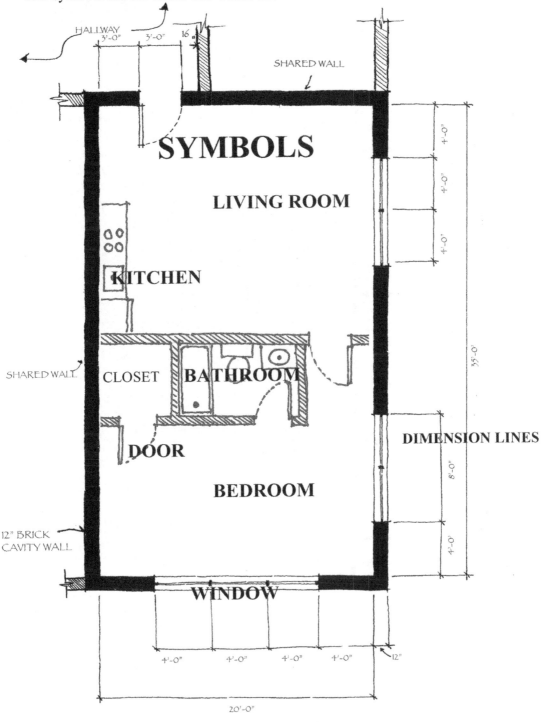

38

HOW ARCHITECTS DRAW PEOPLE.

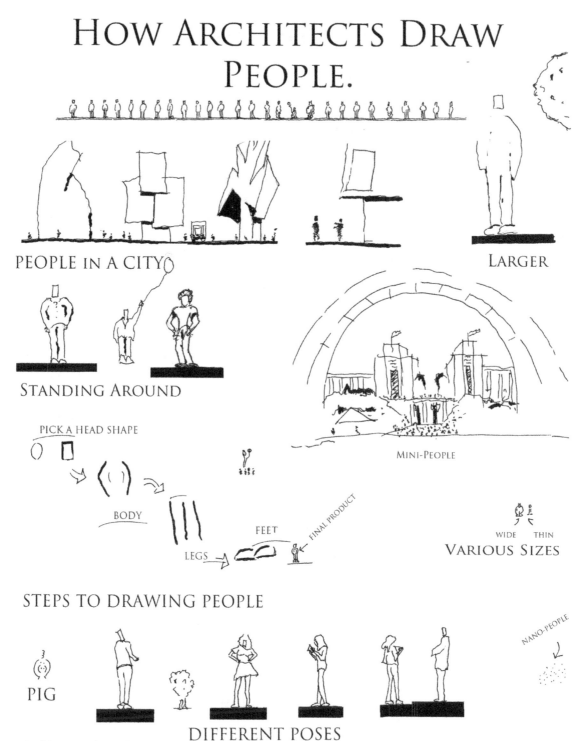

PEOPLE IN A CITY

LARGER

STANDING AROUND

MINI-PEOPLE

PICK A HEAD SHAPE

BODY

FEET

FINAL PRODUCT

LEGS

WIDE   THIN

VARIOUS SIZES

STEPS TO DRAWING PEOPLE

PIG

NANO-PEOPLE

DIFFERENT POSES

Architects and Interior Designers draw all different sized people to fit a drawing's scale. The scale is the size of an object in relation to other items in a drawing. So architects draw people to fit various scales of drawings. People in an architectural drawing help you understand a building's size. You can then imagine yourself standing next to an amazing skyscraper. Try drawing people at all scales.

TIME PERIODS OF ARCHITECTURE

Periods of architecture are the basis of **understanding** world civilizations. Architecture is the foundation of human culture by providing us identifiers of their past.

3400 - 900 BCE Egyptians

850 - 297 BCE Greek

509 - 27 BCE Roman Republic

27 BCE – 410 CE Roman Empire

330 – 1200 Byzantium

700 – 1200 Romanesque / Norman

1100 - 1414 Gothic

1420 – 1580 Renaissance

1518 – 1652 Tudor

1620- 1830 Baroque

1650 – 1790 Rococo

1715 – 1800 Palladian

1789 – 1859 Greek Revival

2778 BCE - Step Pyramid of Zozer Saqqra, Eygpt - Imhotep, 1st named architect

2100 BCE Stonehenge Wiltshire, England

447 BCE Parthenon Columns designed in the simple doric order. Temple to the God Athena. Comissioned by Pericles.

350 BCE Theatre of Epidaurus, Greece, Architect- Polykleitos the Younger

221 BCE the Great Wall Begins Present wall belongs to the Ming Dynasty 14-16 CE Centuries

70 CE The Coloseum, Rome, Italy Elliptical in shape and measures 615 ft (188m) by 510 ft (156m)

120 CE- The Treasury, Petra, Jordan. Capital of the Nabuteans. "Petra" means Rock in Greek

118-128 CE- The Pantheon Rome, Italy

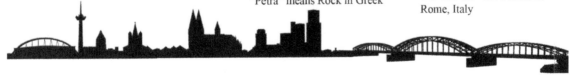

40

1860 – 1900 Arts and Crafts

1890 – 1905 Art Nouveau

1875 – High Rise

1892 – 1910 Prairie Style

1909 – 1919 Italian Futurism

1919 – 1935 Russian Constructivism

1910 – 1920 De Stijl

1919 – 1933 Bauhaus

1920 – 1955 Expressionism

1920 – 1973 Organic Geometry

1918 – 1960 Miesian

1920 – 1960 Modern

1920 -1938 International Style

1952 – 1982 Brutalism

1929 - Skyscraper

1968 – 1990 Post Modern

1978 - 1990 Hi- Tech

1960 – Minimalism

1980 – Deconstruction

1995 - Sustainable

532 -537 Hagia Sofia Istanbul, Turkey, Built by Emperor Justinian. Designed by Isidore of Miletus and Anthemius of Tralles

570- Rock Cut Temple of Elephanta, Mararashta, India

570 Pyramid of the Magician, Uxma, Mexico

670 CE,All Saints Church, Brixworth, Northamptonshire, England

1000 CE- Lingaraja Temple, Bhubaneswar, Orissa, India

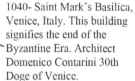

1020- Abbey Church of Mont St. Michel, France. Architect William de Volpiano

1040- Saint Mark's Basilica, Venice, Italy. This building signifies the end of the Byzantine Era. Architect Domenico Contarini 30th Doge of Venice.

Draw an elevation of your house.

An elevation is a view looking straight at an object. Architects draw elevations of each side of building so they can be measured while being constructed. Your challenge is to draw the front of your home. Remember, homes can be houses, apartments, condos, and even mobile.

WHAT A WORLD!

Can you identify all the different countries and their landmarks? All across the earth, countries and their people are identified by landmarks. Many cultures such as Australian Aboriginal people are identified by natural features, like Uluru (Ayers Rock.) However, cities and their inhabitants are recognized by great structures.

1. Circle each landmark with a different color and match below.
2. Match structure with country.

A. Sydney Opera House	____Brazil
B. Petronas Tower	____Mexico
C. Taj Mahal	____Egypt
D. Mount Kilimajaro	____Italy
E. Giza Pyramids	____France
F. Colosseum	____United States of America
G. Saint Basil	____India
H. Effiel Tower	____Malaysia
I. Big Ben	____Tanzania
J. Statue of Liberty	____England
K. USA Capital	____Russia
L. Christ the Redeemer	____China
M. Mayan Pyramids	____Australia
N. Fogong Temple Pagoda	

WHAT A COUNTRY !

From Sea to Shining Sea. The United States is a country full of wonderful sites. See how many you can add in addition to those below.

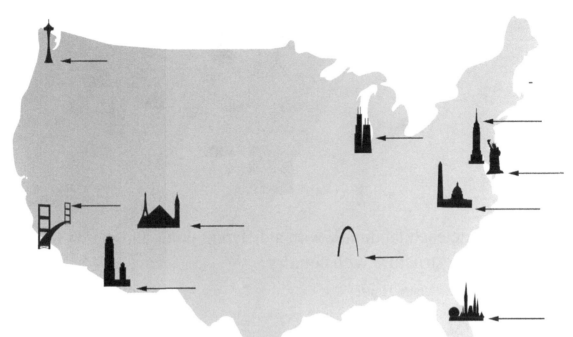

Can you match the landmark with the city?

A. Empire State Building
B. US Capital
C. Willis and Hancock Tower
D. Statue of Liberty   _____
E. Disney World   _____
F. Gateway Arch   _____
G. Las Vegas   _____
H. Golden Gate Bridge   _____
I. Seattle Space Needle   _____
J. Downtown Los Angeles   _____

Designing Cities

Cities are different all over the world. Some are old with ancient buildings and some are brand new. Everyone has an idea for a perfect city. Romans built cities around public areas called forums. Today, cities develop around businesses. People move to cities to find work to support their families. Cities require future planning. Energy, water, and sewer are items that must be designed for growth to accommodate future business and residents. City Planners are people that create rules for were people live, work, and conduct business.

Your new occupation is Chief City Architect.
You are designing a new city based around a central park.
List all the types of buildings your new city will need. Do not forget the police, fireman, and doctors.

_____

_____

_____

_____

_____

_____

_____

_____

_____

_____

_____

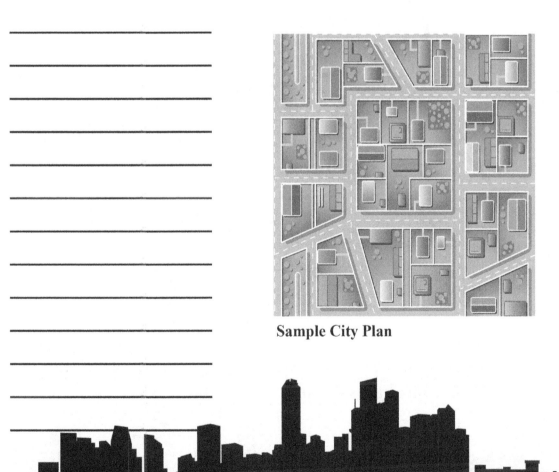

Sample City Plan

THAT IS SO GAUDI

You color
Sagrada Família.

Gaudi didn't color in
the lines, so you don't
have to either.

Antoni Gaudi started the design of the basilica in 1883 and worked until his death in 1926. The Sagrada is scheduled for completion in 2026. The Cathedral is located in Barcelona, Spain.

ANSWER KEY

Page 6
Gladiators battled - Colosseum, Rome
Built with 2.5 - Great Pyramid
It was designed - Colosseum, Rome
Has a hole – Pantheon, Rome
Contains three orders- Colosseum, Rome
Had the largest – Pantheon

Page 7
A. Gothic – Notre Dame de Paris, Paris
B. Byzantine – Hagia Sofia (San Sofia), Istanbul
C. Greek – Parthenon, Athens
D. Roman - Colosseum, Rome

Page 10
Eiffel Tower – Bottom Left
Notre Dame du Haut – Top Right
Týn Church – Top Left
Tower of London – Bottom Right
Leaning Tower of Pisa – Center Right

Page 11
2700 BCE – Imhotep, Step Pyramid
447-438 BCE – Ictinus and Callicrates, Parthenon
118-128 CE – Hadrian, Pantheon

Page 15
Top Left – Islam
Top Right – Christianity
Middle – Judaism
Bottom Left – Buddhism
Bottom Right – Hinduism

Page 16
Left Column – Doric
Middle – Corinthian
Right – Ionic

Page 18
A. Stonehenge – England
B. Great Wall – China
C. Hagia Sofia – Istanbul
D. Castillo – Yucatán Peninsula, Mexico
E. Louvre – France
F. Golden Gate Bridge – San Francisco, USA

Page 22
1. Cathedral
2. Skyscraper
3. School
4. Capitals

Page 25
1. Chicago
2. Egypt
3. St Mark's
4. Eiffel
5. Great Wall
6. Rome
7. Moscow
8. Pisa
9. Ethiopia
10. Nîmes

Page 26
Across 3. Petra
       5. Bauhaus
       6. Monticello
Down 1. Parthenon
      2. Versailles
      3. Pantheon

Page 27
Great Wall of China – Defense
Taj Mahal – Memorial/ Tomb
Lingaraja Temple – Housing
Treasury – Temple / Tomb

Page 33
Less is more
God is in the details

Page 29
India – Taj Mahal
Turkey – Hagia Sofia
Rome – Saint Peters
New York – Empire State
England – Chiswick House
North Carolina – Biltmore House

Page 45
A. Sydney Opera House - Australia
B. Petronas Tower – Malaysia
C. Taj Mahal – India
D. Mount Kilimanjaro – Tanzania
E. Gaza Pyramids – Egypt
F. Colosseum – Italy
G. Saint Basil – Russia
H. Eiffel Tower – France
I. Big Ben – England
J. Statue of Liberty – USA
K. USA Capital – USA
L. Christ the Redeemer – Brazil
M. Mayan Pyramids – Mexico
N. Fogong Temple Pagoda – China

Page 46
A. Empire State Building, New York, New York
B. US Capital – Washington DC
C. Willis and Hancock Tower – Chicago, Illinois
D. Statue of Liberty – New York Harbor, New York
E. Disney World – Orlando, Florida
F. Gateway Arch – St. Louis, Missouri
G. Las Vegas - Nevada
H. Golden Gate Bridge – San Francisco, California
I. Seattle Space Needle – Seattle, Washington
J. Downtown LA, Los Angeles, California

ANSWER KEY

PAGE 7

DO I USE ALL OF THESE BUILDINGS?

Architects throughout time have designed buildings for a specific purpose. Many buildings were for the Gods of Greece. Several were built for Kings and Queens. Today buildings are built for everyone to use. Do you ever use these buildings? Find and circle the building type in the word search.

```
G H L H K K S M V O
A O A O T X K U D N
S U R S N W Y E L N
T S D P T L S S O R
E E I Q C C U O A
L M H T A U R M H B
D G A O Z A K C U
X I A L I M P Z S A
W F C N Z I E J H A
E L F M E T R F T J
```

WORD BANK

Barn	Hospital	School
Castle	House	Skyscraper
Cathedral	Museum	Temple

PAGE 13

Are We Changing Styles Again?

Throughout the history of architecture new styles emerge. People are always looking for the newest and coolest style of the time. However, in the past, the styles did not change as fast as they do today. The Gothic style was used for most Catholic Cathedrals for 800 years. We are still designing building in the Greek styles and that was 2500 years ago.

```
E E B A Z C Q P M G E G
M C O A N R A V F O U N
Z L N B R V W W W T Q U
C Y O A D O R Z M H S V
P B D Q S O Q U L I E V
F P H J C S I U R C N H
D G A O J T I Z E A A D
D K C K N Y Z A K H M H
K O D A K B R M N U O R
V M Z B P K Y K E E R G
C Y H E R F H J Q C R T
B P A L L A D I A N S K
```

Baroque	Gothic	Palladian	Rococo
Byzantium	Greek	Renaissance	Romanesque

PAGE 14

NAME THE PARTS OF THE CATHEDRAL

The Christian cathedral is originally based on the Roman basilicas form. The Roman Basilica was used as a public building normally within the Forum. The Forum was the main section of the city that contained the commercial, government, and religious structures. The cathedral evolved over the centuries, but retained the Roman forms of the nave, aisle, and apse

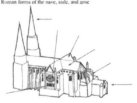

WORD BANK: Spire, Nave, Rose Window, Apse, Transept, Buttress, triforium

PAGE 28

ARCHITECTURAL CAPITALS

```
A W K C Q Y Q L N O D M G R
R M T B X D N O X I T M E K
W A S H I N G T O N L H I X
Q T N N Z U R U Y I B R E S
C B M U Z S I R Y A R W R W
S N O D N O L O X B M R G B
Q Y N C C T H P T R A T M L
M V K U A E E H U A A G W E
H U T I J J O P R S A P V Y
K B R T Y E A N B I W M H Q
K B E N Z L C C M L L Z D K
S N E S R L T S N I O P B H
G A H C B I V F P A R H S U
J G P S I N S V Y V H T F Z
```

Beijing	Brasilia	London	Paris	Rome
Berlin	Canberra	Moscow	Prague	Washington

PAGE 31

Let's Play Follow The Leader

Chartres Cathedral in France has a Labyrinth inlaid in the floor. A labyrinth is like a maze but has only one path from entry to exit. A maze is a game that makes you search for the correct path. Chartres labyrinths has been used as paths for prayer on one's knees.

PAGE 32

I'm trapped and I can't get OUT!

HAMPTON COURT PALACE

Many English gardens have mazes created for entertainment. The oldest surviving hedge maze is at Hampton Court Palace. It was created for King William III in the 17th century.

48

ACTIVITIES INCLUDE word search, mazes, matching, word jumbles, drawing, coloring, name that building, design your own city, and create a floor plan.

Children will learn about architecture, architects, geography, historical landmarks, cities and much more.

© Lemony | Dreamstime.com

FOUNDATIONS IN ARCHITECTURE

Educational products that advance children's understanding of architecture, interior design, and the built environment.

WWW.FOUNDATIONSINARCHITECTURE.COM

Made in the USA
Coppell, TX
29 January 2021